Terrific Learning Themes Clip Art
Creative Clip Art for Popular Classroom Themes

CREDITS
Editors: Carrie Fox & Susan Morris
Layout Design: Lori Jackson

Printed in the USA • All rights reserved.   ISBN 1-59441-359-2

Table of Contents

Introduction & Clip Art Basics

Terrific Learning Themes Clip Art is a compilation of clip art centered around popular learning themes, including the Farm, Community Helpers, Transportation, Weather, the Ocean, and more. Use the black and white images presented in the book to enhance your preschool or early learning themes. Generate unique creations that will meet both decorative and curricular classroom goals and needs. Images from the book are available in both color and black and white on the accompanying CD.

Clip Art Basics

The following are suggestions to help you make theme-based projects using the clip art included in this book and on the CD.

- A good copy machine is essential for creating any clip art project. Use a copier's enlargement or reduction functions when making copies from the book. Use a fine-tip black marker to personalize clip art pieces or template copies.
- To create your own project, copy, resize, and cut the clip art as needed to create accents for bulletin boards, newsletters, or for use in theme-based centers. Images can also be used for art projects, story starters, accents to label with student names, or student work displays.

Using the CD

Create projects in black and white or color using the CD! As you open the CD on your computer, follow the prompts to find the images you need and the program you want to use. Images from the book can be found easily by using the file name listed below each image. Choose either the color or black and white images folder, then choose an image's file name from the alphabetical list. The CD contains step-by-step directions for placing the clip art images into many different classroom publishing programs. All images on the CD are sized for optimal clarity but can be reduced to meet your clip art needs.

Using the color images can save you valuable time, while using the black and white images can encourage students' creativity. Whatever your classroom objectives require, the clip art included in this book will make your classroom projects fun and original!

farm_animals_header

barn_window

barn1

barn2

barn3

4

farmer_tractor

farmer1

farmer2

farmer3

farmer4

farm_dog1

farm_dog2

farm_dog_family

farm_dog3

feed

haystack

5

horseshoe

donkey1

horse1

horse2

horse3

horse4

horses

horse5

donkey2

cows

cow1

llama1

bull1

bull2

cow2

llama2

cow_calf1

cow_calf2

sheep1

sheep2

sheep_family1

sheep_family2

sheep3

goat1

goat_family1

goat2

goat_family2

goat3

goose1

goose2

gosling

goose3

chicken

swan

chick

chicken_family

chicken_egg

9

turkey1

duckling

duck1

turkey3

turkey2

turkey_poults

turkey_poult

duck2

duck_pond

10

pig_tractor

pig1

pig2

pig_family1

pig_family2

rabbit1

rabbit2

trough

11

hay_bale

scarecrow1

scarecrow_kids

crow

fall_harvest

scarecrow2

mice_in_hay

12

Community Helpers

community_header

grocery_bag

egg

steak

grocery_shopper

butter

cookie

bread

grocer

candy

cash_register

apple1

carrots

nuts_and_beans

13

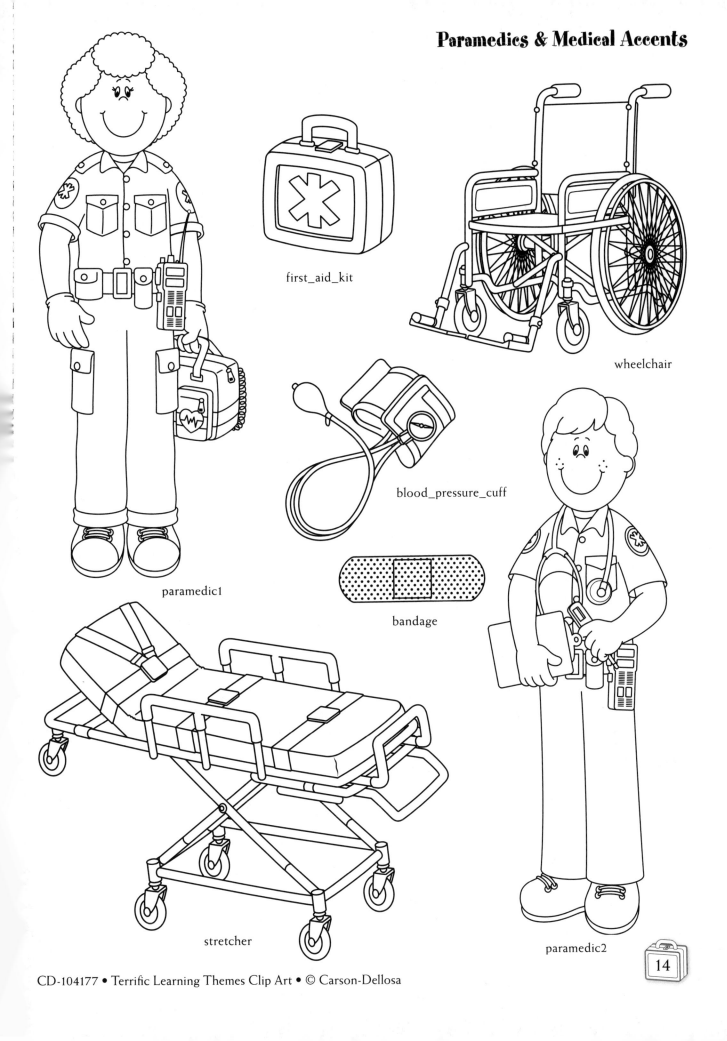

first_aid_kit

wheelchair

blood_pressure_cuff

bandage

paramedic1

stretcher

paramedic2

14

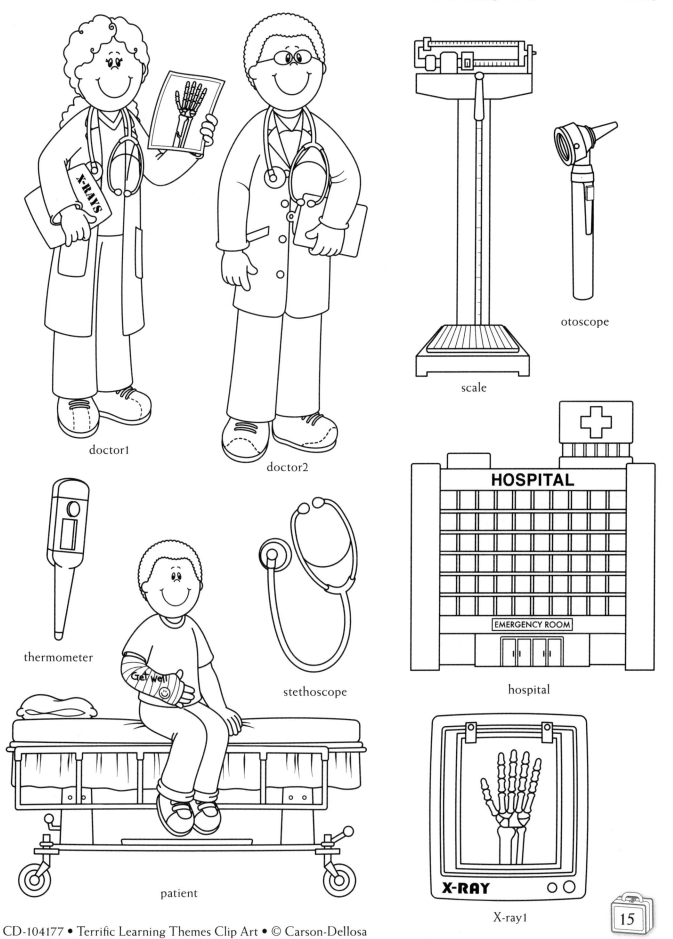

Doctors & Medical Accents

doctor1

doctor2

scale

otoscope

thermometer

patient

stethoscope

HOSPITAL

EMERGENCY ROOM

hospital

X-RAY

X-ray1

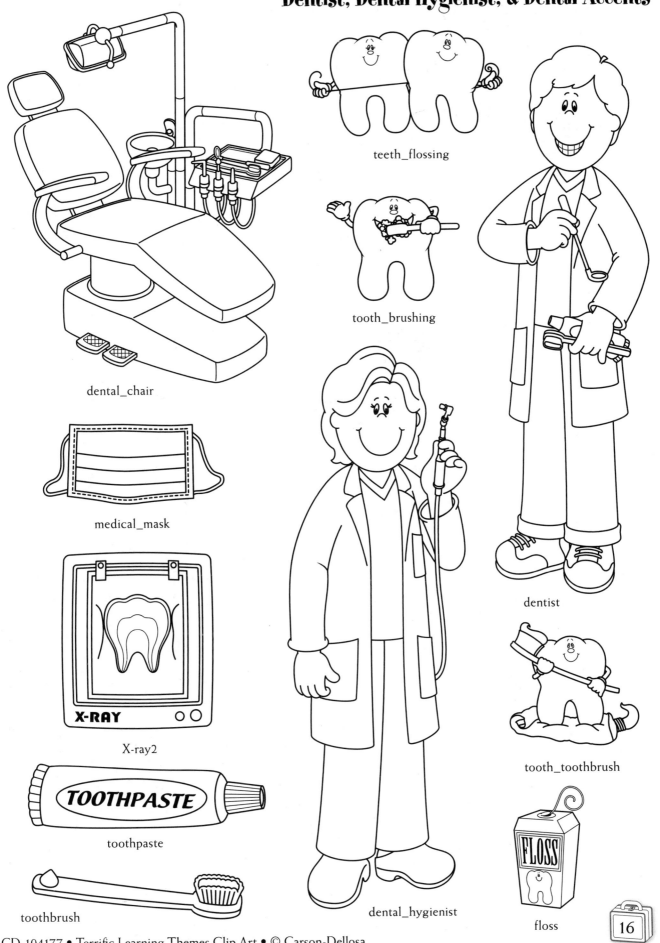

Dentist, Dental Hygienist, & Dental Accents

teeth_flossing

tooth_brushing

dental_chair

medical_mask

X-RAY

X-ray2

TOOTHPASTE

toothpaste

toothbrush

dentist

dental_hygienist

tooth_toothbrush

FLOSS

floss

16

veterinarian1

vet_technician

veterinarian2

chameleon

rabbit3

dog1

cat

dog2

kids_with_pets

gavel

judge

jury_box

judge_bench

JUDGE

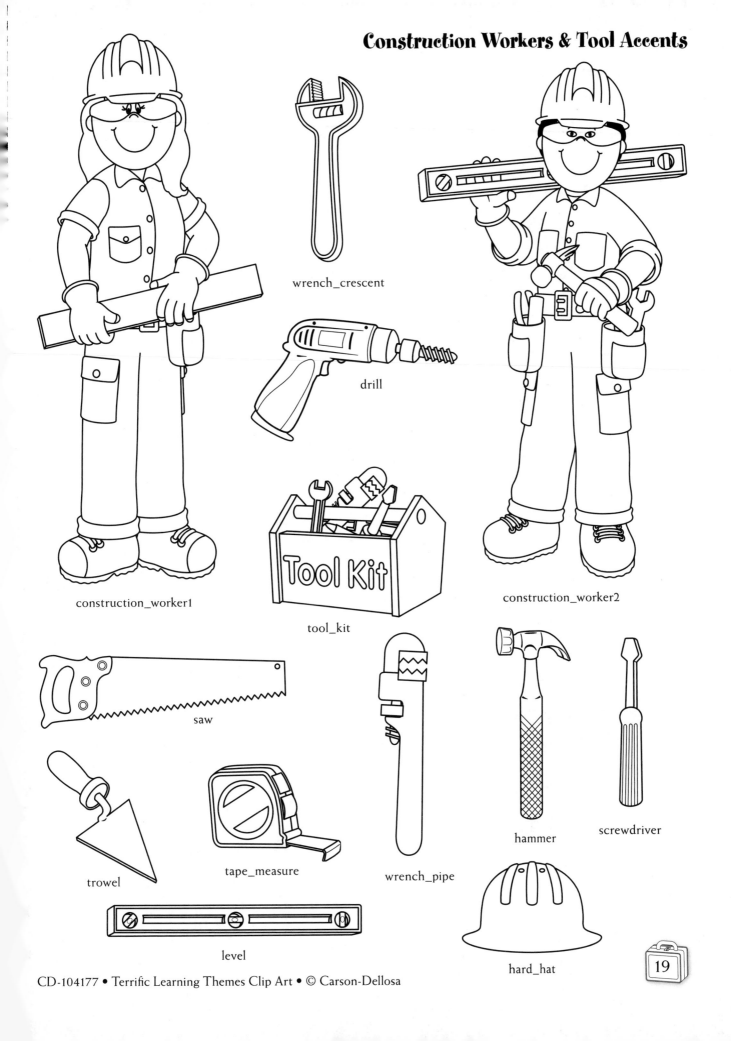

Construction Workers & Tool Accents

wrench_crescent

drill

construction_worker1

tool_kit

construction_worker2

saw

trowel

tape_measure

wrench_pipe

hammer

screwdriver

level

hard_hat

CD-104177 • Terrific Learning Themes Clip Art • © Carson-Dellosa

package

stamp1

stamp2

letter_dog

mailbox2

mail_carrier

mailbox1

postcard

mailbox3

mailbag

envelope

20

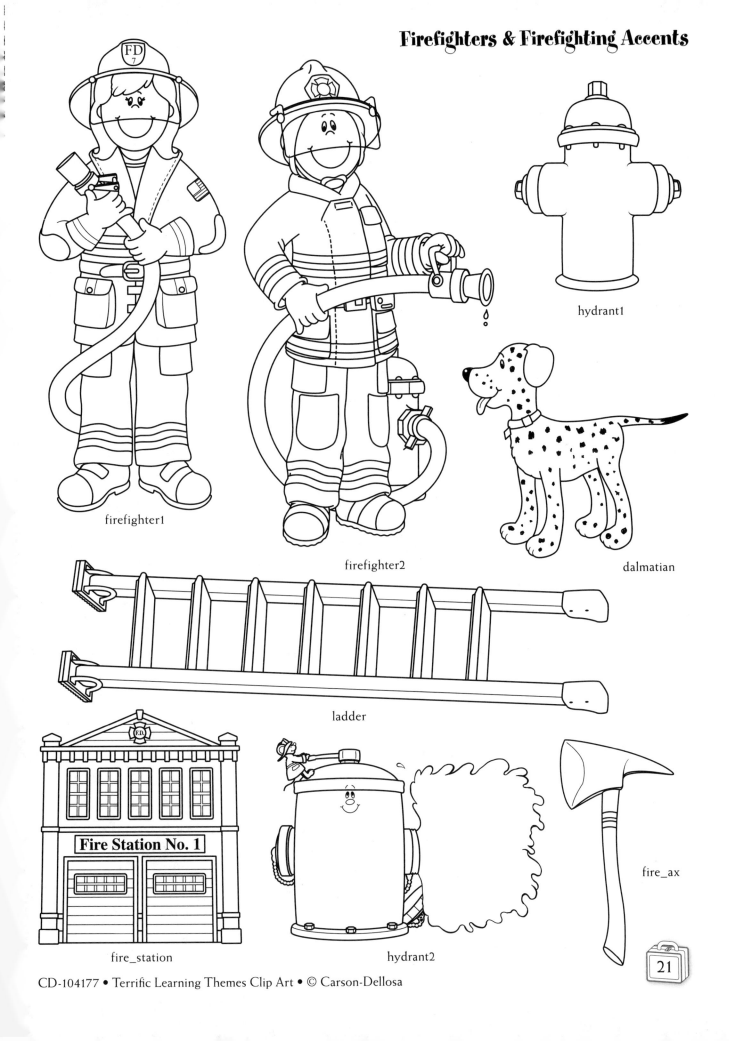

firefighter1

firefighter2

hydrant1

dalmatian

ladder

Fire Station No. 1

fire_station

hydrant2

fire_ax

21

globe

pencil

teacher1

school

teacher2

apple2

notepad

#1 IN-BOX

chalkboard

teacher_desk

22

books1

book1

computer

book2

books2

librarian1

bookshelf

librarian2

23

TV_camera

camera

microphone

radio

TV_cameraperson

TV_reporter

television

newspaper

DAILY NEWS

24

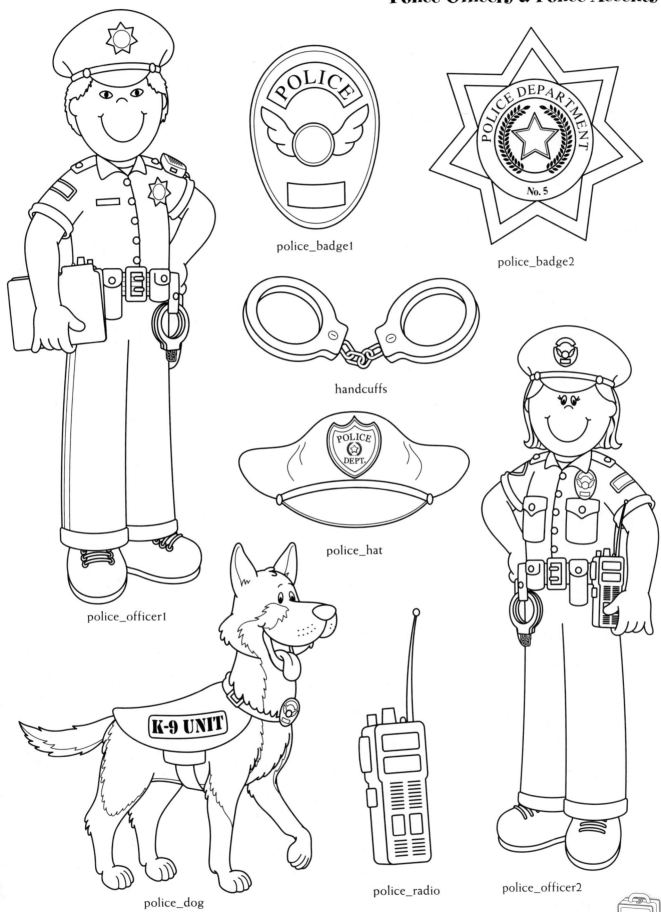

police_badge1

police_badge2

handcuffs

police_hat

police_officer1

police_dog

police_radio

police_officer2

25

CITY TRANSIT AUTHORITY BUS PASS

bus_ticket

bus_driver1

bus_driver2

chef

ladle

can_opener

pot_holder

pot

frying_pan

26

hair_dryer

hairbrush

scissors

hairstylist

clipboard

PLAN #2

football

sports_cone

coach

soccer_ball

tennis_ball

baseball

27

transportation_header

train_ticket_booth

train_engine

train_conductor

train_car1

train_car2

train_car3

train_car4

train_car5

train_car6

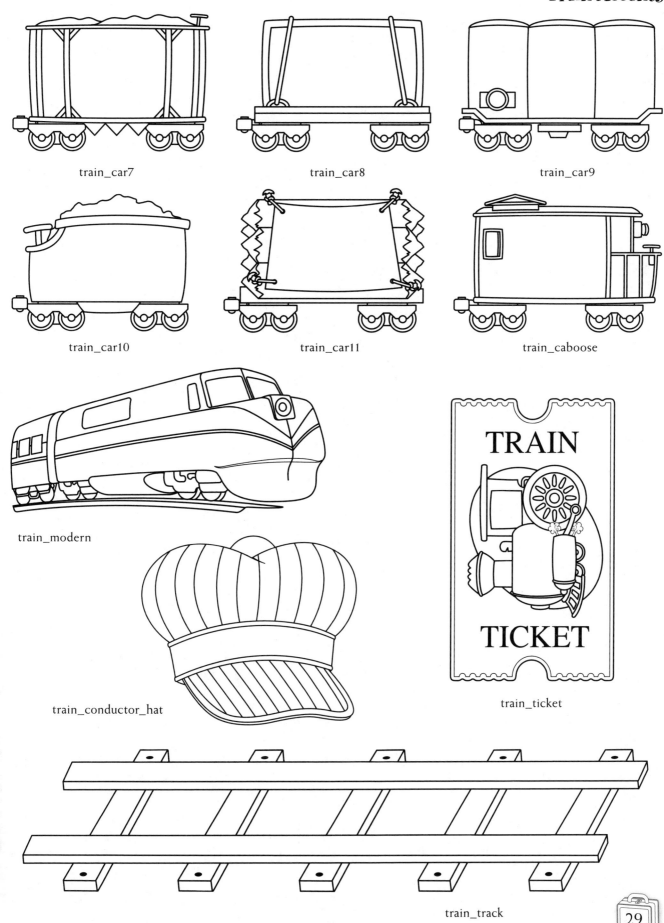

train_car7

train_car8

train_car9

train_car10

train_car11

train_caboose

train_modern

TRAIN

TICKET

train_conductor_hat

train_ticket

train_track

29

airplane1

airplane2

hot_air_balloon

blimp

helicopter

space_shuttle

airplane3

airplane4

dump_truck

bulldozer

fire_engine

van

motorcycle

police_car

bicycle

city_bus

TV_van

car

ambulance

taxi

cement_truck

crane

school_bus

cruise_ship

sailboat

canoe

ship

life_jacket

inflatable_raft

tugboat

motorboat

33

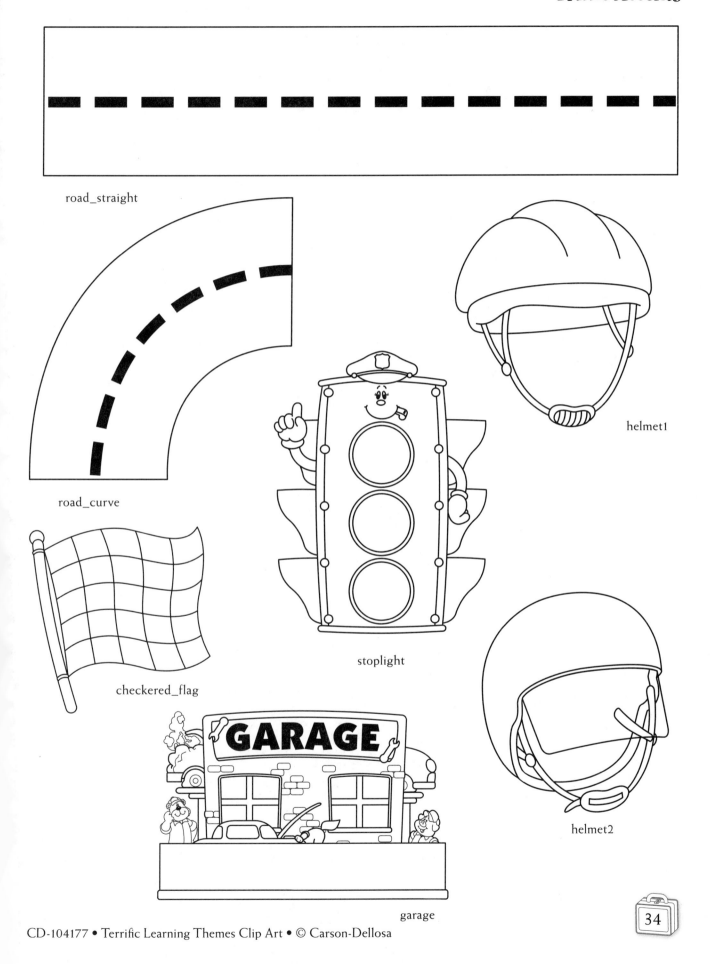

road_straight

road_curve

helmet1

checkered_flag

stoplight

helmet2

GARAGE

garage

34

weather_header

sun1

sun2

sun3

sun4

sun5

35

cloud1

rainbow

rain

cloud2

raindrop

cloud3

rain_cloud

cloud4

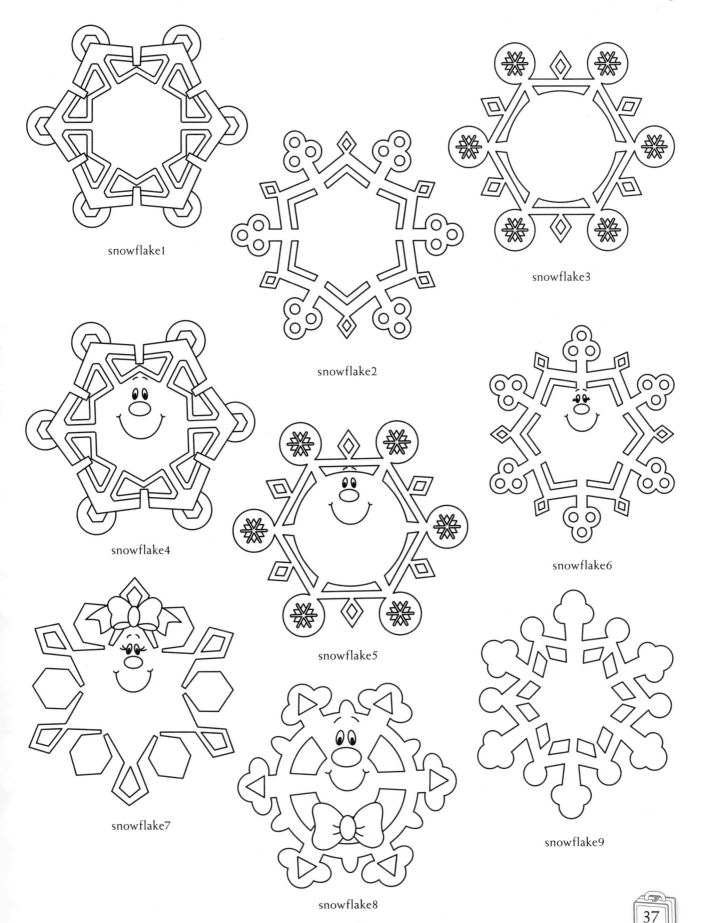

snowflake1

snowflake2

snowflake3

snowflake4

snowflake5

snowflake6

snowflake7

snowflake8

snowflake9

bear_jeans

bear_sunglasses

bear_sunscreen

bear_sun_visor

weather_bear

bear_Hawaiian_shirt

bear_smile_shirt

bear_winter_coat

bear_winter_hat

bear_scarf

bear_winter_boots

bear_mitten1

bear_mitten2

bear_rain_hat

bear_umbrella

bear_rain_boots

bear_raincoat

39

rainy_header

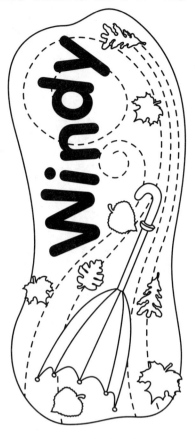

windy_header

snowy_header

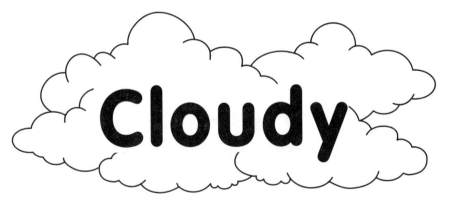

cloudy_header

foggy_header

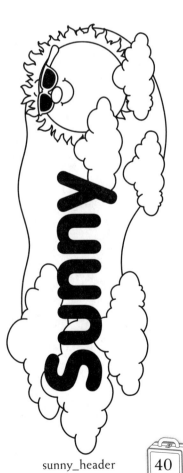

sunny_header

40

CD-104177 • Terrific Learning Themes Clip Art • © Carson-Dellosa

ocean_header

diver1

diver2

diver_dog

diver3

treasure_chest

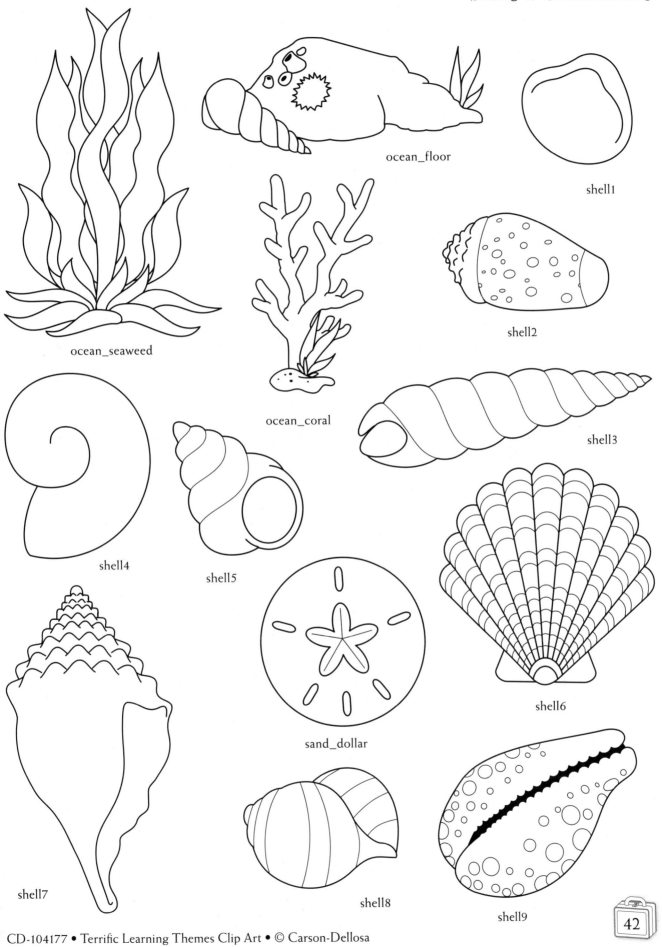

Shells & Ocean Plants

ocean_floor

shell1

ocean_seaweed

shell2

ocean_coral

shell3

shell4

shell5

shell6

sand_dollar

shell7

shell8

shell9

42

CD-104177 • Terrific Learning Themes Clip Art • © Carson-Dellosa

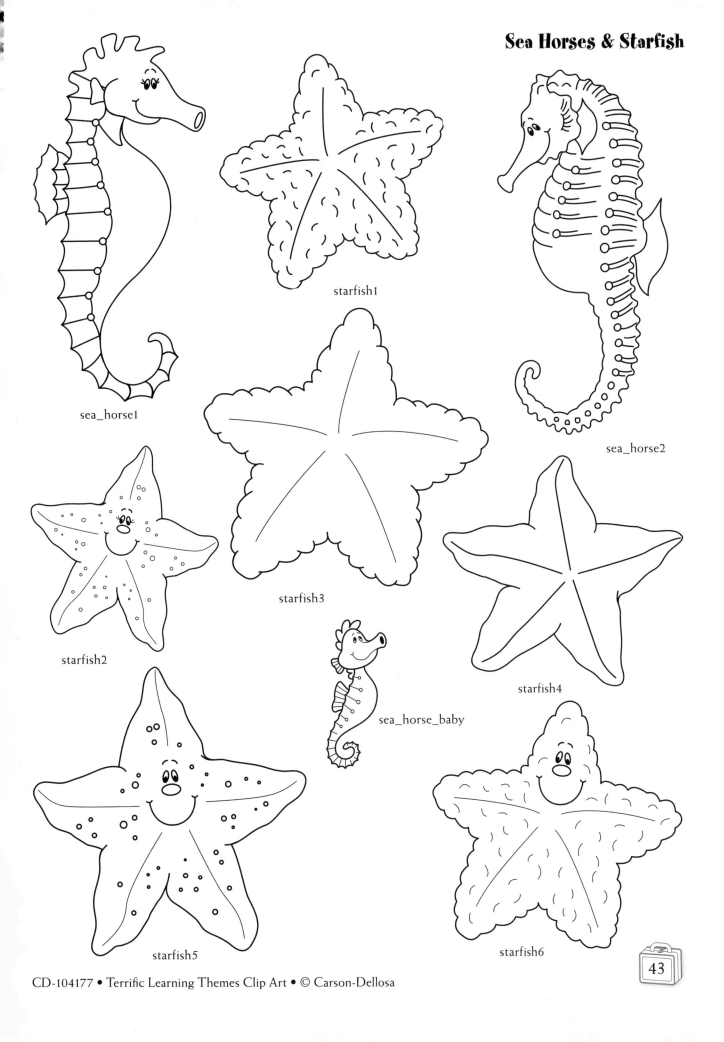

starfish1

sea_horse1

sea_horse2

starfish2

starfish3

starfish4

sea_horse_baby

starfish5

starfish6

fishing_rod1

sand_pail1

rowboat1

sand_pail2

fishing_net

rowboat2

sand_castle

boat_oar

shovel

fishing_rod2

fish1

fish2

fish3

fish4

fish5

fish6

fish7

fish8

fish9

fish10

fish_school

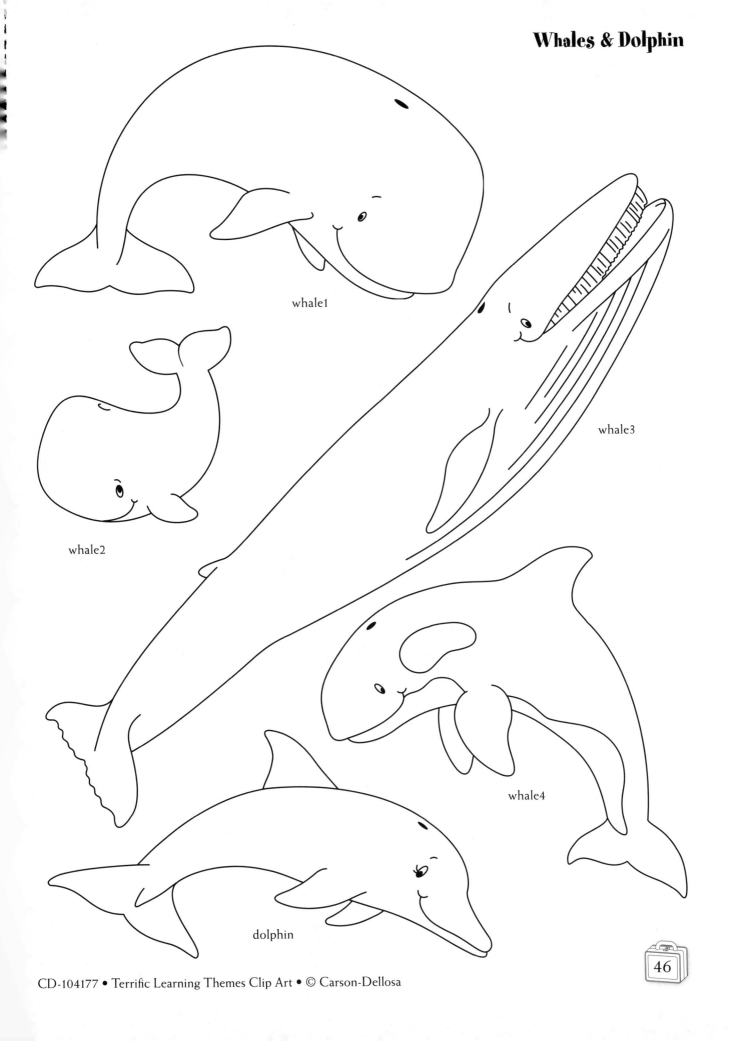

whale1

whale2

whale3

whale4

dolphin

46

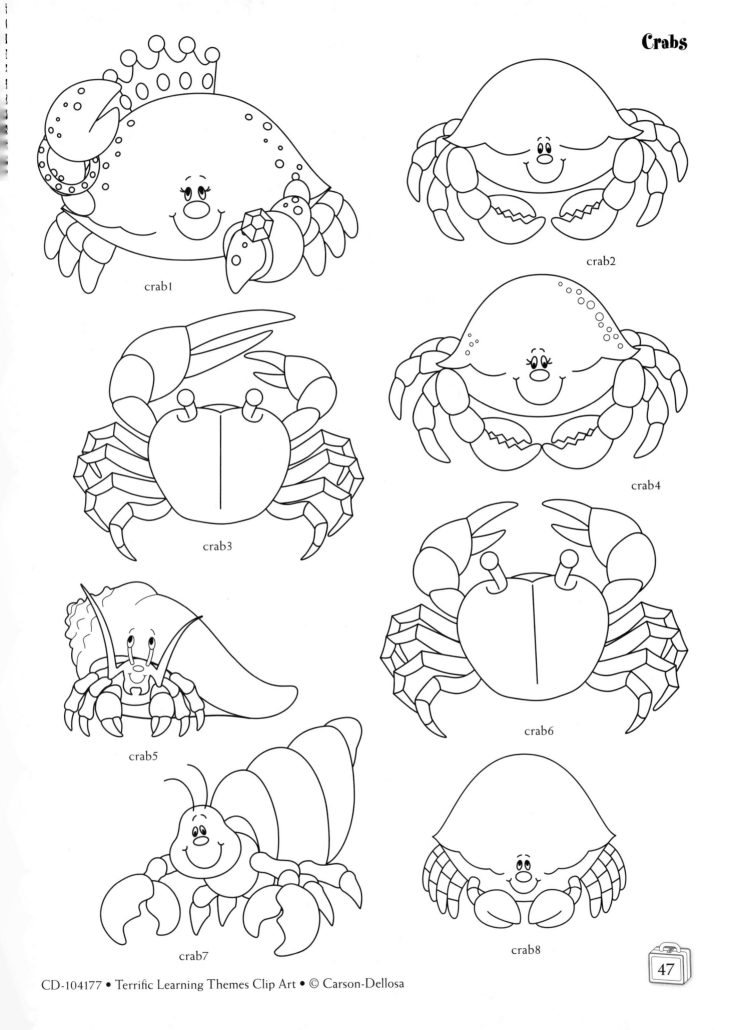

crab1

crab2

crab3

crab4

crab5

crab6

crab7

crab8

shark1

shark2

ray1

shark3

shark4

shark5

ray2

shark6

octopus1

octopus2

octopus3

octopus4

octopus5

octopus6

fish_header

sea_anemone

jellyfish

oyster

underwater_scene1

sea_turtle

underwater_scene2

50

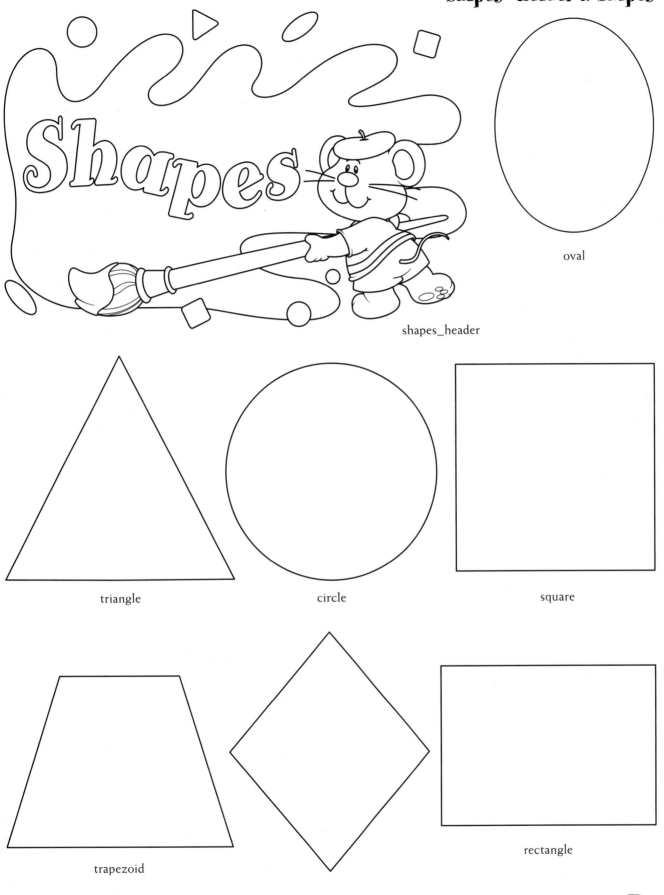

oval

shapes_header

triangle

circle

square

trapezoid

rhombus

rectangle

rectangle

rectangle_text

triangle

triangle_text

hexagon

hexagon_text

circle

circle_text

square

square_text

oval

oval_text

trapezoid

trapezoid_text

rhombus

rhombus_text

octagon

octagon_text

hexagon

octagon

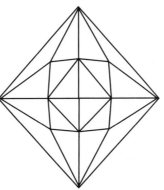

rectangle_door

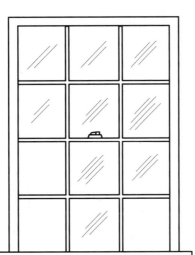

rectangle_window

oval_frame

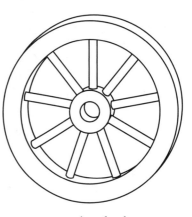

circle_wheel

rhombus_jewel

52

triangle_pizza

square_cracker

oval_rug

square_disc

circle_clock

octagon_sign

rhombus_sign

trapezoid_pyramid

hexagon_canister

53

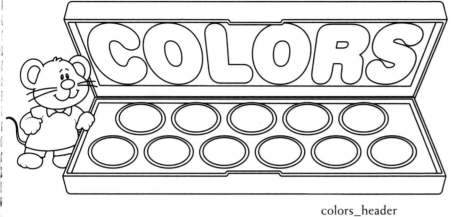

colors_header

paint_palette1

color_word_orange

color_word_yellow

purple

color_word_purple

blue

color_word_blue

green

color_word_green

gray

color_word_gray

white

color_word_white

pink

color_word_pink

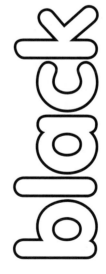

color_word_black

brown

color_word_brown

red

color_word_red

color_football

color_elephant

color_heart

color_apple

color_bird

color_ribbon

color_eggplant

color_cloud

color_grapes

color_spider

color_star

color_pumpkin

color_clover

color_frog

color_pig

color_mouse_pink

color_mouse_orange

color_mouse_gray

color_mouse_green

color_mouse_yellow

color_crow

color_mouse_red

color_mouse_blue

color_mouse_brown

color_mouse

color_dog

color_snowflake

color_chick

paint_palette2

color_mouse_black

color_carrot

color_mouse_purple

color_mouse_white

57

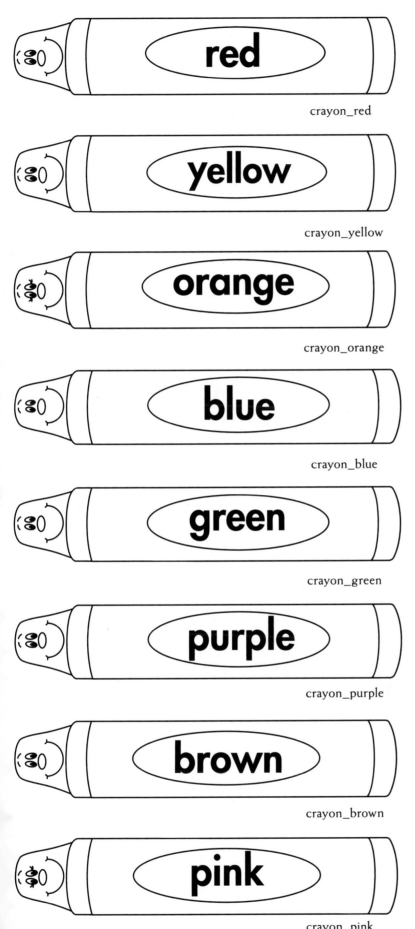

red

crayon_red

yellow

crayon_yellow

orange

crayon_orange

blue

crayon_blue

green

crayon_green

purple

crayon_purple

brown

crayon_brown

pink

crayon_pink

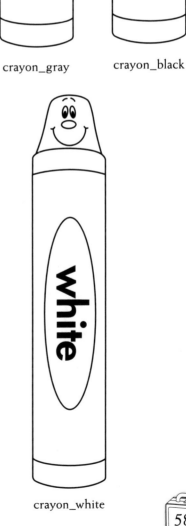

gray

crayon_gray

black

crayon_black

white

crayon_white

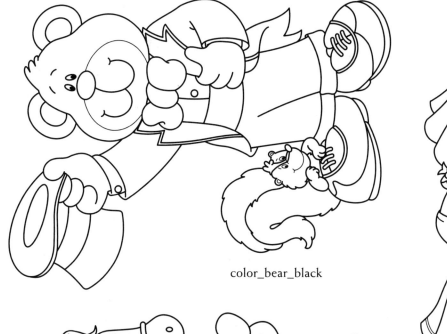

color_bear_black

color_bear_white

color_bear_brown

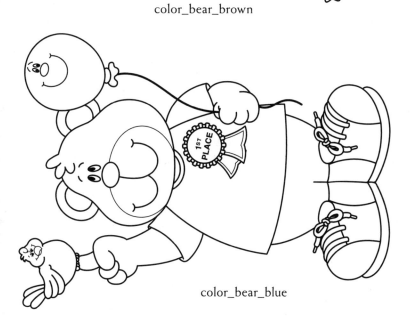

color_bear_blue

color_bear_purple

59

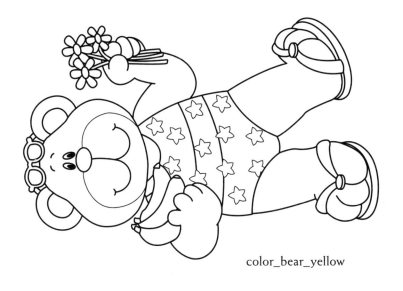

color_bear_yellow

color_bear_pink

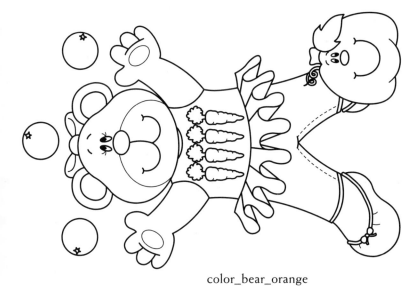

color_bear_orange

color_bear_green

color_bear_red

60

all_about_me_header

grow_up

favorite_book

favorite_subject

favorite_sport

My Pet

my_pet

My Favorite Food

favorite_food

My Favorite Color

favorite_color

My Favorite TV Show

favorite_show

My Photo

my_photo

I Really Enjoy

I_enjoy

62

my_home

My Friends

my_friends

my_school

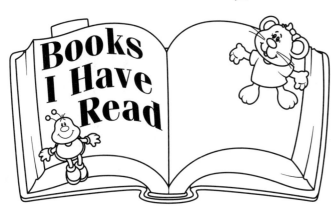

books_read

busy_bees

my_birthday

pencil_writing

CD-104177 • Terrific Learning Themes Clip Art • © Carson-Dellosa

ribbon1

ribbon_star_student

ribbon2

ribbon3

ribbon_birthday

ribbon_first_place

ribbon_second_place

ribbon_third_place